A Conversation with John H. Shenefield

A Conversation with John H. Shenefield

Held on October 6, 1978
at the American Enterprise Institute for Public Policy Research
Washington, D.C.

ISBN 0–8447–3336–9

Library of Congress Catalog Card No. 79–50686

AEI Studies 233

Printed in the United States of America

Introduction

Soon after John Shenefield was confirmed as assistant attorney general for antitrust last year, the *National Journal* described him as an outsider, by Washington standards. Even then, he was certainly no stranger to antitrust litigation, however. A 1965 graduate of the Harvard Law School, Mr. Shenefield practiced antitrust law for the next twelve years with the Richmond, Virginia, firm of Hunton and Williams. He is the author of numerous articles on antitrust law, including the Annual Survey of Antitrust Developments for the *Washington and Lee Law Review* for several years running. Between 1975 and 1977 he also taught courses on economic regulation at the University of Richmond Law School.

Mr. Shenefield has taken over the Antitrust Division at what is undoubtedly an unusually challenging time for that office. Academic critics have lately become more vocal in their insistence that antitrust actions are too often motivated by blind hatred of bigness, rather than a reasoned consideration of competitiveness and efficiency. At the same time, the Supreme Court has indicated that it will now scrutinize antitrust cases more closely than in earlier decades, giving more weight to straight economic analysis than to the broad social theories often invoked in the past.

Mr. Shenefield, himself, has urged less regulation and more reliance on market forces in many public statements, endorsing the Interstate Commerce Commission's deregulation of trucking, for example, and supporting airline deregulation in testimony. He has conceded in a recent interview, however, that, beyond economic analysis and legal precedent, the Antitrust Division draws inspiration for its choice of actions from the populist tradition from which the antitrust laws derived. Many critics charge that eagerness to maintain a populist image, rather than any well-reasoned concern for market competition, has prompted the Antitrust Division to pursue cases on such novel theories as shared monopoly and indirect price signaling. These theories are so vague and confused, according to some critics, that they might be used to characterize even the most competitive market situations.

Mr. Shenefield has announced his determination to pursue big cases that will test the limits of the law, but he has stressed that every effort should be made to focus on conceptual issues and to avoid disputes about the factual record, which have dragged out many other big cases for more than a decade. Though he has argued that the IBM case, which has now cost the government $7 million and nine years of effort, is definitely worth continuing, Mr. Shenefield has stated his willingness to ask Congress for new legislation should the courts refuse to uphold some of the controversial theories on which present antitrust actions are planned.

In any event, Mr. Shenefield's undeniably ambitious course since taking office, and his eagerness to focus public discussion on basic principles of antitrust regulation, make this exchange with antitrust scholars and other experts particularly interesting and fruitful.

JAMES C. MILLER III
American Enterprise Institute

A Conversation with John H. Shenefield

I was asked to give a broad-brush treatment of the Antitrust Division, my own interests and emphases, and perhaps a look into the new fiscal year. I thought I could do that best by painting a picture of the division as I saw it when I arrived, and by recounting the ways I think I have made, or will make, a difference.

I do so with a sense of modesty, because the division, in my view, has always had a reputation as a first-class group of lawyers. It has always had an important mission, and it has a proud record. I do not pretend, nor would I be able to persuade anyone, that I will make a major difference in any of those areas.

I did find, however, certain areas of possible improvement. First, I found a division that lacked the tools and organization to be a first-class litigating unit in the twentieth century, in big cases. The management of a litigation team and of the litigation support tools is a hidden aspect of law enforcement and of litigation success that does not receive much attention in the newspapers. But, as any of our litigators will confirm, management is extremely important to the lawyers who must go into court.

Second, I saw an agency that had fulfilled its traditional role of prosecuting price-fixing cases and had more recently focused on horizontal merger cases. It had been very successful in these areas: price-fixing convictions are now virtually automatic, and horizontal mergers, of the most direct kind, are becoming rarer and rarer.

Third, I saw a division that had broken new ground in the area of regulatory filings. It had attempted to introduce the notion of competition in regulated industries; to argue persuasively in support of this notion in appearances before regulatory commissions, before Congress, and within the executive branch; and then, of course, to assist Congress in the production of deregulation legislation.

In broad and general terms, that was the division as I saw it. It seemed to me that improvement was desirable in several areas: first, in management; second, in the area of concentrated industries, what Dr. Miller alluded to as "shared monopoly"; third, in the broadening and enrichment of merger law; fourth, in the extension of deregulation efforts to parts of the regulated sector that, while they had been discussed in the academic world, had not yet received much attention in Washington, or at least not in the Antitrust Division. I include here the energy area in particular.

Finally, it seemed to me that our major monopolization cases—IBM and AT&T—were in need of a close look. Obviously, I will not be able to go into details about either one of those cases this afternoon, but suffice it to say that each has had its close look. Some changes have been made in the organization of each case, and other modifications will gradually follow as the litigation unfolds.

Let me now fill in some of the broad brush strokes of this brief overview and set the stage for questions and further discussion. The division has about 425 lawyers and about 45 or 50 professional economists on the staff, about 350 of whom can expect to appear in court at some time during the year. That is a large law firm, by any standards.

That law firm, in the spring of 1977, did not have the benefit of an adequate law library. Its law library would not have been accredited in any law school in this country by the American Bar Association. Nor did the division have the benefit of adequate litigation support—by that, I mean the use of a computer for document retrieval, information organization, economic research, legal research. The result was that the division found itself at a significant disadvantage in courtrooms against firms that did have those benefits and those advantages. In my former firm, for example, cases with 15,000 documents or more qualified for automatic data processing support. In the division, extra support was given on an ad hoc basis and was not ever considered until the number of documents rose to 120,000 to 150,000, at which time it might well be too late in a specific case.

In addition, there was no way for a lawyer in one section to have access, other than by word of mouth, to the work product in any other part of the division. Research that was done on a point of law, say, in one section on the AT&T case, might not be available to or even known about in the judgment enforcement section across the street or in some other section downstairs.

Furthermore, the use of paralegals, now common in any major litigating firm, was very limited. The ratio of paralegals to lawyers in the division, when I arrived there, was one to eight. That, as any litigator recognizes, is simply not an adequate balance. It is now about one to four, which is about where it should stay if we are going to be engaged in very many large cases.

We rearranged the sections, putting energy in a single section rather than in two separate sections as it had been before. We changed some people, and we made organizational changes. For example, we took negotiations of judgments out of one section and made that section responsible for judgment enforcement. There were a variety of changes of that sort, all of them designed to support the mission in a more efficient way.

I mentioned shared monopoly. When I spoke in passing of the division's historic role in prosecuting price-fixing, I did in no way deprecate it as an unimportant mission. It is very important. Anything I say here should not be taken as suggesting any reorientation away from it. Indeed, in a recent speech about voluntary informers, I emphasized our activity in price-fixing and our efforts to hold out a carrot as well as a stick, and, if possible, to accomplish even more in the area using no more resources. But to say that price-fixing is important and that we intend to continue working on it by no means exhausts the subject of the applicability of Section 1 of the Sherman Act. We also think that is important, which is why we are looking very closely at shared monopoly.

The premise is that some concentrated industries in this country are performing in a less than competitive way, and that they do so in a variety of ways that we do not fully understand at this point. We need to look at them very closely indeed. Dr. Miller mentioned price signaling, but that is a very small part of a much larger picture. The symptoms that one observes are the absence of price competition, or the lack of innovation, or inadequate performance on any of several indices of noncompetitive activity within an industry.

In a variety of ways, such as the use of coordinating devices, firms within those industries have engaged in a form of collusion, even if it has not involved explicit conspiracy of the classic Section 1 variety. I would mention for illustrative purposes the distribution and wide circulation of price books which announce price protection plans. These are designed to reassure customers that no lower prices will be offered, but, in fact, are probably also designed to convey to competitors the message that it would be of no advantage to them to cut their prices.

We have proceeded to analyze this phenomenon in two ways. First, we took a quick look at about twenty industries that our Economics Policy Office and those of us who had been thinking about the problem had selected as possible candidates. It has already been made public that included in this group are the steel, iron ore, and aluminum industries, but I will not name any others this afternoon.

A more comprehensive second stage of the approach involved analyzing each of the most concentrated industries in the country; matching those with a profile of each industry; developing a Sherman Act history of our enforcement, if any, in those industries; and distributing those histories to the relevant commodity sections within the division. I have on my desk—or will soon have—a selection of those industries that seem to offer the highest probability for our success in bringing cases, along with a game plan for how to proceed with respect to each. We will make a number of decisions about the order of investigation and priorities.

I mentioned horizontal mergers and alluded to the need to enrich, to broaden, to push out the boundaries of the merger law. My perception is that the courts are unduly conservative, not simply in the way they look at competitive aspects but in their blindness to anticompetitive aspects of certain mergers of conglomerates. If the courts are going to live up to their professed interest in looking at the actual competitive realities and the actual economic situation in each case, they must go beyond traditional competition theory and look at a whole new theory that is evolving—for the lack of a better word, conglomerate theory. That is given particular force by my impression that there will be an enormous number of mergers in the next two or three months. Every sign points in that direction. I leave it to all of you to consider why it is happening now, and from what particular companies we ought to be looking for some merger activity. It is clearly beginning; the daily headlines are filled with it, and I see no sign of its abating. In fact, I see signs of its intensifying.

What do I mean when I talk about enriching a theory of merger law? It seems to me that the conglomerate theories that Judge McLaren used as a basis for litigation in the first part of the Nixon administration deserve a better ventilation than they received at the appellate court level at that time. In some situations they make very good sense indeed. Obviously, they are not a substitute for close analysis of particular situations, but the ideas of potential competition, entrenchment, and reciprocity do not seem to have been given fair consideration in the appellate courts. My guess is that if they are presented with the right fact situations in well-litigated cases, the appellate courts will see the sense of those arguments. If not, it would be appropriate to present the issue to Congress. Without litigation at some level of the courts, it seems to me unlikely that the Congress would greet any such presentation affirmatively. Whether or not it has been litigated, Congress and the American people ought to be dealing with the question whether they want concentration to stay at its present level, to increase, or to decrease. What sorts of mergers, if any, does the public want to forbid outright? Does it want to save certain kinds of mergers, if efficiencies or economies of certain kinds are demonstrated? And who ought to be the judge in those cases, who ought to be the decision maker?

These seem to be at least as much political and social questions as they are economic questions. I would not accede to the statements of some critics that the Antitrust Division is engaged in bringing cases that do not make good economic sense. I would like to ask which cases they had in mind and talk about them, if they are past cases.

So, we will be looking at conglomerate mergers, or mergers that go slightly beyond the standard kind of mechanical market analysis, and in the right kinds of fact situation we will be bringing cases.

I mentioned that we would continue to emphasize accelerating our regulatory filings. That is a shorthand way of saying we will be involved with the regulatory agencies, which seems to have been one of the areas in which the Antitrust Division has been clearly productive. I assume I would not find much disagreement on this point, except, perhaps, from a chairman of a regulatory agency. The effects of the efforts at the Civil Aeronautics Board are in no doubt, and my hope is that no less will shortly be seen at the Interstate Commerce Commission. I have high hopes in other areas, as well.

It seemed to me that the Antitrust Division, for one reason or another, had not been adequately involved in energy over the years—although that is not true as a blanket statement. It had been involved in the electric utility industry to a major extent, under the 1970 amendments to the Atomic Energy Act. Something like 80 percent of the electric power in this country is generated under a license condition that was either imposed in the proceedings of the Atomic Energy Commission—now the Nuclear Regulatory Commission—or negotiated through the leverage offered by those hearings. But that leaves a wide variety of energy topics that have not received the kind of intensive competition analysis that bore fruit in actual litigation filings.

We have tried to organize our efforts to do more of that kind of analysis. We have engaged in a substantial number of filings in the Department of Energy, and we will continue to do that. We are concerned that energy regulations already on the books—and others still to come, presumably—may be at least as anticompetitive as private restraints could ever be. It is important to focus on that issue and to take it fully into account when those regulations are put on the books. We propose to raise those questions in the appropriate forum, insofar as our resources permit us to do so.

That is a very quick look at the Antitrust Division.

Questions and Answers

PAUL MACAVOY, professor of economics, Yale University: I might have a large number of questions about the economic analytical foundations of either of the two major thrusts in the direction of shared monopoly cases or the conglomeration policies you espoused. Let me try to express those questions with respect to the shared monopoly policy that is in the offing.

There have been about a hundred articles that have appeared in the economic research journals since the Neil Task Force Report, which tried to summarize what we knew at that time about shared monopoly. The main—perhaps even the massive—thrust of these journal articles is that, through the best of scientific procedures, economists can find no relationship between high levels of concentration and noncompetitive market performance. This research includes the last six articles to come from the Federal Trade Commission's senior staff by people such as John Kwoka and Michael Klass; six articles of the same nature by Edward McCarthy Miller of the National Transport Safety Board; and other articles that have appeared in journals such as *Political Economy* and *Econometrica*. It seems fair to say that, if we were to poll from one end of Massachusetts Avenue to the other, we could not find three out of a hundred economists who would argue that there is an analytical foundation for your proceeding, particularly since the entire research literature supports the opposite view that a shared monopoly reduction scheme should not begin by looking at the highly concentrated industries.

Why is it that, in that vast law firm, you have managed to get started in that direction without referring to this economic research base at all?

MR. SHENEFIELD: I would not presume to debate with you which way the economic literature points. I am not sure that I am as confident as you are that all economists agree on that or on anything else. I would be surprised if they did. It would be contrary to my own personal experience to find unanimity in that profession on anything. But I would be willing to accept that from one end of Massachusetts Avenue to the other economists are of the view, as I heard you state the proposition, that there is no necessary correlation between concentration and lack of competitive performance.

I assume we may not mean quite the same thing by shared monopoly. By shared monopoly, obviously, I have reference to the economic results, but in the legal sense I also have reference to the available law under which we must proceed, and I must take account of likelihood of success under that law, when the problem is viewed from any one of a number of different angles.

The law I refer to is Section 1 and Section 2 of the Sherman Act. Section 1 is a statute that covers conspiracy or contract and seems to speak in terms of communication or a meeting of the minds. Section 2 deals with a conspiracy to monopolize or an attempt at monopolization and speaks more in terms of structure. If we assume that there is a problem of shared monopoly, the approach that offers the most hope of success, in a litigative context, is the Section 1 approach. That does not mean that there are not other shared monopolies in other kinds of industries. It means only that if we find a shared monopoly in a concentrated industry, experience teaches us that we are more likely to find the facts under Section 1 than under Section 2. I tried to illustrate that with the example of the price books and price communication. The approach we adopt represents less a conclusion that there is a correlation and more a legal and litigation judgment that, where we find shared monopolies, we are more likely to be able to deal with them adequately through Section 1 than through Section 2.

That does not make the director of Congress Watch, Mark Green, happy. He regards that as a monument to timid decision making, or something of the sort. I think that he and others who agree with him mean that there may well be some promise in Section 2 as well. Perhaps in that case some of the literature to which you allude would be helpful and would obviously be informative; I don't know.

We are proposing to develop approaches under Section 2. I regard those as much harder and, therefore, we have not emphasized those as much, but they will come along in due course. If we should see something of the nature of a shared monopoly that concerned us and that could be reached better under Section 2 than Section 1, we might try that approach.

PROFESSOR MACAVOY: Without persisting, I hope, too far on this, I put it the way I did because early on you made some very interesting remarks about how to manage a law firm. They at least implied the need to allocate scarce resources, lawyers' resources. As an economist, I am not yet willing to admit value to lawyers' resources, but—[Laughter.]

MR. SHENEFIELD: As a lawyer, I am frequently not willing to admit it, either, certainly not in the marketplace.

PROFESSOR MACAVOY: But since resources are limited and since lawyers can work on alternative case sets, one thing you said bothered me. You implied a flow chart from high concentration, to aspects of performance, and then to serious case investigation of an industry, and the first arrow went from high concentration to noncompetitive performance. I do not contribute to this literature, but I teach it in class, and I just cannot find that arrow. It really seems to have disappeared in the last ten years.

MR. SHENEFIELD: Would you state that there is the reverse of a correlation?

PROFESSOR MACAVOY: You would find no real correlation.

GEORGE EADS, Rand Corporation: If a man goes duck hunting, he tries to find out where to look for the ducks, and he looks for them in the concentrated area more than in the unconcentrated area.

PROFESSOR MACAVOY: That doesn't work. The literature doesn't say that.

MR. SHENEFIELD: It doesn't say we are more likely to find them there, but neither does it say we will find the total absence of them.

PROFESSOR MACAVOY: That is right.

MR. SHENEFIELD: As long as I am looking in one place or another, I would rather shoot with the rifle that is going to work. That is all I am really saying.

RICHARD ZECKHAUSER, professor of political economy, Harvard University: In any case, there are plenty of concentrated areas.

PROFESSOR MACAVOY: You can win cases anywhere.

MR. SHENEFIELD: No. Section 2 does not offer me the kind of help that Section 1 does.

PROFESSOR MACAVOY: If you are looking for a Section 1 case by going to a highly concentrated industry, you might have some help—there are some basic theoretical foundations for doing that. But in a Section 1 case the files indicate concerted action and intent; in a Section 2 case the price behavior, per se, is not competitive. I just do not find in the research literature that highly concentrated industries generate a statistically significant cause-effect relationship with noncompetitive market performance.

MR. SHENEFIELD: Let me say what I think in a slightly different way. The possible result of all of this effort may be no cases at all, so that you may be quite right. Although the literature does not say so, it might turn out that there is not only the absence of correlation but the reverse—an inverse correlation. I may find nothing, and in that event we won't file any case. We are not going to file cases merely to improve our totals.

PROFESSOR MACAVOY: As a footnote on that, Robert Bork argues in a recent book that industries are highly concentrated because of highly effective competition among them, generating all the advantages from scale and high rates of growth.

MR. SHENEFIELD: Does the economic literature support that?

PROFESSOR MACAVOY: That is only a hypothesis at this stage.

DR. MILLER: Sam Peltzman, the editor of the *Journal of Political Economy*, has just published an important article in the *Journal of Law and Economics* in which he concludes that deconcentration would have rather substantial negative effects on prices. He wants to ask a question.

SAM PELTZMAN, professor of business economics, University of Chicago: I was not entirely sure what you were saying about the resurrection of the McLaren notions on conglomerates and the need for new legislation. At what point do his notions become inadequate and when does the need for new legislation become impelling? Specifically, do you feel there may be a need for new legislation because of the lack of ability to apply anticompetitive rules to conglomerates? Do you feel you may have to attack the problem directly and say, "It is really a matter of size, itself," for whatever reason? If so, are you then willing to spell out how much economic advantage you would be willing to tolerate for that sake? That is about three questions.

MR. SHENEFIELD: Let me try to respond, and then you can ask follow-up questions to refine my answer a bit.

I was saying a couple of things. First of all, I think the issue of what kinds of mergers and what sorts of law enforcement are to be permitted in this country by law—whether made by the judicial or the legislative branch—is something that ought to be discussed publicly. It is not something that the judges or I ought to be thinking about all by ourselves. It is a peculiarly political and social question that goes beyond the points that you were making, which is why the legislature ought to be considering proposals on this aspect of antitrust law. That is one point.

The second point is purely a matter of tactics in the enactment of law. If new legislation is necessary on any ground, we cannot argue for new law if we have not tried out the old law. As you know, Judge McLaren's filed cases had generally negative acceptance at the district court level, but they were rarely appealed and, when appealed, the results were inconclusive. They therefore have not been given a thorough viewing at the appellate court level and certainly not at the Supreme Court level. If there is a necessity, on any ground, for legislation, it seems to me, as a matter of tactics, we at least have to try the conglomerate theories.

Third, we may not incur much economic harm by forbidding certain kinds of mergers. The economic literature to which I have access is less than totally satisfactory here. But we do know that there are not many mergers among the largest of all manufacturing companies. If, for instance, a statute said that in the absence of clear demonstration of efficiencies of some sort, no company in the top 200 manufacturing firms could merge with any other in the top 200, it might not do much economic harm because there would not be very many such mergers. In addition, the justifications normally given for mergers might be peculiarly inapplicable in those kinds of situations. Such firms are large enough already to have access to technology or capital and all the normal kinds of efficiencies. There is no need for managements to be concerned about selling out. So there may not be harm of the sort that you address.

Now, that's three answers. I don't know whether they match your three questions.

PROFESSOR PELTZMAN: Your answers tell me that you are seeking legislation which focuses on size, but there is an economic test also involved.

MR. SHENEFIELD: Under our present law—as I have said in testimony—we cannot bring cases that do not make economic sense. And I am committed not to do that.

Aggregate concentration, for instance, is a theme that is frequently sounded in certain sectors of the antitrust community. It is said that certain companies should not be allowed to merge because they are just too large. I might even agree with that. I am inclined in that direction, although I would like to know a good deal more about what sorts of harm that kind of a statute would produce. But that is not a theory that I think we can push responsibly under Section 7 of the Clayton Act.

I do not believe we are disabled by pushing theories of entrenchment, or potential competition, or reciprocity because in the proper fact situations these tendencies can be shown to do economic harm of the traditional kind. It requires, in my view, a more sensitive analysis and a greater willingness to follow the theory of economics and less concern with what can actually be proven in court. I might therefore be interested in two procedural changes: one, some sort of reversal of the burden of proof; and, two, some kind of adjustment in the schedule by which we are currently moving to trial.

I think the way mergers are currently being tried will have a significant effect on the way the law develops. It is interesting that in moving toward more efficient litigation and in applying the so-called Hart-Scott-Rodino premerger notification, which gives us an automatic stay for thirty days, we are probably going to be getting to the trial of merger cases much sooner, on average, than we did before. We may well be out of the business of seeking preliminary injunctions. The use of precomplaint discovery—which was conferred on us in 1974—means we will not have time to develop major fact reservoirs and to perfect theories. We will know about the merger when we are notified about it, and three days later we are going to have to move one way or the other.

A second difference is that the Supreme Court, in the *General Dynamics* case,[1] has given a new shape to merger trials. Not only do we have to look at the guidelines, but we also have to evaluate the facts behind the guidelines. The precise defense of a merger that is to be offered will never be known until the complaint is filed, but if the

[1] United States v. General Dynamics, 415 U.S. 486 (1974).

trial is held ten or fifteen days after the complaint is filed, there will be no discovery on the nature of the defense, so that we are engaged in speculation.

These two differences may mean that the balance, which was to have been tilted more in the government's favor, may now, in fact, tilt the other way somewhat. The premerger notification procedures became effective September 5, and I don't believe we have filed a merger case since then, so we are not quite sure how it will work. But that is the concern I have.

RODERICK HILLS, former chairman of the Securities and Exchange Commission: Let me retreat to your dialogue with Paul MacAvoy and see if I understand it. I am really concerned only about my lack of understanding.

The premise is that you are interested in shared monopoly cases and that the priorities have been established for concentrated industries. Paul MacAvoy commented that there is no price behavior data, of which he is aware, that would justify choosing concentrated industries for your review. He challenged your allocation of priorities. I take it, from what you said, that you might accept that fact, but that you would look in the concentrated industries because you would expect to find better evidence of something else. That is, I thought you said that even if there are no price data that would justify going to concentrated industries, nonetheless you might concentrate in those industries because you would be more likely to find conspiracies or collusion of some sort.

MR. SHENEFIELD: I understand shared monopoly is a result, and I understand there are a variety of ways in which that result can be achieved. Some of those ways can be grounds for suits under Section 1 and some under Section 2. I understood MacAvoy's point to be that the result is no more likely to be found in those industries that could be sued under Section 1 than in those that could be sued under Section 2, but that the result is necessarily no *less* likely to be found.

PROFESSOR MACAVOY: You can look anywhere for Section 1 violation. A collective organization and a conspiracy in restraint of trade can be found among five shepherds or among five steel manufacturers. It is more likely, in theory, to be found in the highly concentrated industries because the chances are greater that the cartel will work there. They just don't do this for the fun of it. You therefore look for the smoking gun, for the memoranda with the same date and the same address in the upper right-hand corner, and you obtain the evidence necessary to win a Section 1 case through intent to conspire.

I would put your people to work on the concentrated industries because they might find a few more there than from a random selection of industries, according to four-digit categories. The question is, however, will they find noncompetitive price behavior in terms of increased price-cost margins, higher levels of profitability, extra normal rates of return, more discrimination, more price inflexibility, and a lower level of research and development in new product and service quality performance in those industries with high concentration? That may well be a Section 2 issue,[2] if Section 2 can be stretched enough to get Alcoa-like standards for a finding of monopolizing.

I am saying that if you set your people to work looking for that in the highly concentrated industries, there may be thirty to forty articles in good journals which say they are not going to find it. It is essentially a fruitless strategy.

MR. SHENEFIELD: That is different from what you said before. I thought you said there was an absence of correlation.

PROFESSOR MACAVOY: There is no correlation between these measures of noncompetitive performance that I have just designated and a measure of market structure which you call "high concentration."

MR. SHENEFIELD: I don't know what the journals say, but my economists should and, I presume, do. If that is wrong, then either I need new economists or they can't read.

PROFESSOR MACAVOY: They are producing some of it. They are responsible for some of these articles.

MR. SHENEFIELD: We seem to be missing the distinction between the result and what happens when we find the result. I understand you to say that there is no greater likelihood of those results in Section 1 reachable areas than in Section 2 areas.

PROFESSOR MACAVOY: That is too technical a response for me.

MR. SHENEFIELD: Unfortunately, we are trying to bridge a gap between two professions. Let me try to finish my response. My concern is that when I find these results I be able to do something about them. My

[2] United States v. Aluminum Company of America, 148 F.2d 416 (2d Cir. 1945).

judgment is that if I find them in areas which can be reached by Section 2, it will not do me much good. But if I can find them in areas that can be reached by Section 1—and I believe I can—then I will be able to do something about it. That is the only reason we have pursued Section 1 first rather than second. It hasn't much to do with the theory of it.

MR. HILLS: Are you less likely to find those indications of poor social behavior in concentrated industries than in less concentrated industries?

PROFESSOR MACAVOY: Neither less nor more.

PROFESSOR ZECKHAUSER: Even if it were less, your argument might still apply.

MR. SHENEFIELD: It might still apply.

CALVIN COLLIER, former chairman, Federal Trade Commission: Well, you would have to conduct fewer depositions. [Laughter.]

PROFESSOR MACAVOY: More employees buried in the bowels of larger corporations means more depositions.

MR. COLLIER: I have a question about mergers. You indicated that some of Judge McLaren's theories of conglomeration were not tested. But there have been a lot of cases brought by government agencies claiming potential competition loss, either perceived or actual, and, in fact, the courts have not been very receptive to those cases, aside from the *Phillips* case[3] by the Antitrust Division and a couple of others. The decisions have almost all been adverse to the government in these cases of potential competition, whether they alleged perceived potential or actual potential theories.

Similarly, there are a lot of cases that seemed to rely on the notion of entrenchment, whatever it is these days, and the notion of reciprocity, which also does not seem to be a very economically coherent notion. I don't think many economists would indicate that reciprocity is a very coherent idea. But the point is, you indicated that those theories have not been tried. It is my impression that they have been tried and either have not been successful or have been randomly

[3] United States v. Phillips Petroleum Company, 367 Fed. Supp. 1226 (Central District of California, 1973); affirmed 418 U.S. 906 (1974).

successful and randomly unsuccessful. Since *Marine Bancorporation*,[4] they have been generally unsuccessful all across the board. There have been a lot of prosecutions on those theories in the last three years.

MR. SHENEFIELD: No, there really have not been. In the area of potential competition, the Supreme Court has expressly reserved half of the doctrine and expressly never decided it.

You are right, the more recent cases have not been particularly well received. The Supreme Court will moderate its views over time, presumably, one way or the other. It is possible, I think, responsibly to read *Marine Bancorp.* and *Connecticut Bank*[5] as cases that have more to do with regulated industries than, perhaps, with potential competition. There were clear barriers to entry, having to do with state lincensing, and the kind of potential competition that occurs in a normal manufacturing context simply was not there. Justice Powell, in *Marine Bancorp.*, was, I think, quite right to draw that distinction.

I suppose *Procter & Gamble*[6] is the highest court's decision on entrenchment. I thought it endorsed the idea, rather than anything else, but it has not been tried very much in recent years.

MR. COLLIER: That might be related in part to your earlier statement that the Antitrust Division tries not to bring cases that don't make sense.

MR. SHENEFIELD: No, I don't think so, but there are different views of what makes economic sense. I would not agree that the entrenchment theory does not sometimes make economic sense, would you?

MR. COLLIER: I don't know what it means these days.

MR. SHENEFIELD: Let me give you an example of what it means. When a very large national firm acquires a dominant firm in a concentrated industry, the merger is presumed to entrench that leading firm and make it less likely that competition will be brought into the industry either by new entrants or through a foothold or toehold merger.

MR. COLLIER: That does not explain why the acquiring firm is so successful once it gets into the industry. You say that it will be hard to

4 United States v. Marine Bancorporation, Inc., 418 U.S. 602 (1974).

5 United States v. Connecticut National Bank, 418 U.S. 656 (1974).

6 Federal Trade Commission v. Procter & Gamble Co., 386 U.S. 568 (1967).

dislodge a new giant that enters an industry composed of midgets. But why would it be hard to dislodge the firm if it is not serving consumers well?

MR. SHENEFIELD: We start off with a dominant firm in a group of midgets, as you put it. It is a small group, and they are not terribly competitive for whatever reason. All of a sudden, a much larger firm acquires the dominant firm.

It can be argued that it would be better, more competitive, if that acquiring firm, say, Phillip Morris, were to take over the sixth largest firm and not the largest. Maybe it was more competitive for Phillip Morris to acquire Miller's instead of Budweiser. I suppose we could argue about that. My own intuition on that point is that it probably was a little more competitive. The question is whether we ought to have a theory that prevents the acquisition of the number one firm and aids the acquisition of the number six firm, because there might be some competitive difference there. That is what the entrenchment theory is about, and it makes pretty good intuitive sense to me, though I am not an economist.

MR. COLLIER: The theory tends to equate the size of a firm with its success as a competitor in a market.

MR. SHENEFIELD: The size pre-exists its arrival and makes its arrival peculiarly significant, given the small size of the others.

MR. COLLIER: I do not mean to argue with theory I do not understand, but rather to suggest that these various theories have been used in merger enforcement in the past three or four years with mixed results —with admittedly poor results from the government's standpoint in the last three years, probably since *Marine Bancorp*. Whatever the Antitrust Division's position is, the courts don't seem to regard it as uniquely a regulated industry's precedent.

DR. EADS: Are you arguing that we should take it to the Congress now, then?

MR. COLLIER: I have a concern about basing new merger policy on an assumption that the theories have not been tested, when it seems to me many of them have.

MR. SHENEFIELD: I don't agree that they have been tested very recently.

MR. HILLS: In the example of the beer industry, it seems to me facile to talk in terms of the first or sixth largest firm.

MR. SHENEFIELD: I used that example because it was an actual fact situation we could look at.

MR. HILLS: I appreciate that. But if we try to decide why Miller's has overtaken the four other companies in the beer industry we see that it has not cut into the Budweiser or Anheuser Busch share of the market at all. It has managed to take away from all the smaller firms a greater share of the market than has Anheuser Busch, but there has been no lessening of the market share of Anheuser Busch. Indeed, Anheuser Busch now has a larger share than before. Why is that? Was it merely because a big company got a smaller company? Did that big company donate capital to the smaller one, or give it a good marketing person? Did it hire a better advertising agency? It strikes me that these kinds of guidelines are terribly dangerous.

MR. SHENEFIELD: I was trying to make clear what the entrenchment theory would encourage and discourage. The entrenchment theory applies to acquiring the dominant firm in a concentrated industry and, thus, would have discouraged Phillip Morris from acquiring Budweiser, or Anheuser Busch, but would have assisted it in acquiring the sixth or seventh largest firm.

MR. HILLS: It assumes that something happened that is relevant. From the little I know about that particular group, however, that is not so at all, not even if a smaller company did the acquiring. It was really more a question of advertising technique and marketing technique and was not allocation of capital. Indeed, if Phillip Morris had taken over the largest firm, it might have lost a share of the market.

MR. SHENEFIELD: Peter Stroh's brewery doesn't think that is right, I gather, from reading about its losses in the newspaper.

MR. HILLS: Well, he is not an economist, either. [Laughter.]

MR. SHENEFIELD: Fortunately, not everybody is an economist.

PROFESSOR MACAVOY: Your mechanism works if the acquiring firm brings economic, financial, or political power into the industry from outside to bolster number six or number one. What is that doughy substance that is brought in and that provides the boost? Unless it is there, then Mr. Hills is right. It is just a random process of purchase and sale.

MR. SHENEFIELD: I guess I need an economics tutorial, because that is not clear to me at all. If I had a choice, I would rather have Phillip Morris acquire the number six firm.

PROFESSOR MACAVOY: Because you think Phillip Morris is going to bring something into the industry that will push number six up and unsettle numbers five through one.

DR. EADS: It is also because Phillip Morris believes that it will get something from the merger. It is not just saying, "I want to buy a beer firm today."

PROFESSOR MACAVOY: There is a range of other reasons, and Phillip Morris does not necessarily believe that it is bringing economic power into the market.

MR. COLLIER: Phillip Morris bought Miller's, not one of the others. I don't know whether it thought the government would prevent it from buying one of the others, but why should its choice be prescribed? If it wants to buy one, two, three, four, five, or six, why shouldn't that decision be given the benefit of the doubt? Why should that choice be second-guessed just because the acquiring firm is coming in from the outside?

MR. SHENEFIELD: If an outside firm buys number six, it triggers performance by numbers one through five that was not there before. If it is allowed to acquire number one, it may or may not trigger that kind of response to number six. It might have been quite content to remain the dominant firm in the industry.

MR. COLLIER: It was Phillip Morris's choice to buy number six, not the government's choice. And its choice may have had something to do with its success. The point is, why should the government force it to buy number six if it prefers to enter the industry by acquiring number one?

MR. SHENEFIELD: I think we are saying the same thing over and over.

PROFESSOR ZECKHAUSER: If number one is bought, it would, in some sense, get bigger with more money behind it, and the industry would become more concentrated, as was the case described by Mr. Hills. In fact, number six grew up to be number two, and the two top firms controlled more of the market.

If Anheuser Busch was initially the most powerful firm within the industry, it may have pushed out its market share as much as it could. At first sight, an equally good theory within economics is that it will be more anticompetitive to buy the number six firm. Let's assume that all we want to do is intervene: We will lose more competition by letting it buy the number six firm than by letting it buy number one. I am not advancing that as another theory, but certainly the facts that were described are consistent with that.

The point I want to make is that it is really very dangerous to sit around and speculate. Most of the people at this table who are economists have been burned at least four or five times by asking themselves how a particular industry will work. They conjecture a bit, they write something down, and they may even come up with a theoretical model. Then they go out and look at the facts, and they say, "Damn, we had a terrific article, but the world doesn't work out that way."

I think you may be at that stage, on this theory at least, and the only difference between you and the economists is that when you take action it matters. [Laughter.]

DR. EADS: It is merely being suggested here that consideration be given to bringing some fairly clear-cut cases to trial. A lot of us who were involved in the McLaren thing felt very unsatisfied. Those cases were not well done and not pursued; I don't know about the most recent cases. Trying to find some good vehicles in order to see whether or not the law applies, and, if it does not apply, seeing about getting it changed—that does not seem to me a thing we should worry about.

PROFESSOR MACAVOY: We should worry.

MR. HILLS: There is an underlying assumption in this whole discussion that somehow bringing more economic strength into a market where there are few competitors is necessarily relevant. Sure, it might be relevant sometimes. My own interpretation is that in some of the conglomerate cases, particularly in the beer industry, economic strength had nothing to do with it at all. It was irrelevant that Phillip Morris had a lot of economic strength. What bothers me is not what has been said about this case or any other case, but the unspoken assumption that is not being challenged. The assumption is that it is relevant that a large company, with lots of cash and lots of bank loans, picks up a company in a concentrated sort of way. The beer industry is concentrated and becoming more concentrated every day, but it is assumed that because Phillip Morris is large it probably should not acquire a beer company, whereas maybe a smaller firm could. It is too easy to assume that a large company brings something to the small area merely because it has financial strength.

Mr. Shenefield: Let me respond to that in two ways. Some people do argue that Phillip Morris should not be allowed to go into the beer industry at all. As I understand the public record, it is argued that Phillip Morris is using profits from its cigarettes to subsidize its activities in the beer industry—that Miller's rate of advertising is much higher than any other company in the beer industry. I don't know whether that is true or not. It isn't really important, because I was not making that proposition. The proposition I was making is that, left to a choice as to which firm Phillip Morris should acquire, I have a preference, which may or may not be based rationally in economic doctrine, though I would like to explore it further. In a concentrated industry with a not particularly active or innovative competitive group of firms, I would prefer Phillip Morris to acquire a relatively small firm rather than the dominant, largest one. I believe that would produce, in sum, a more competitive performance, and in order to achieve this I would be willing to forgo the benefits of letting Phillip Morris make its own judgment totally unhindered.

Mr. Hills: Let me proclaim the facts that are known. The beer industry is less competitive, it is more concentrated, the profit margins are higher, and the other firms are less able to compete because of Phillip Morris's presence. That is what has happened.

Mr. Shenefield: I don't know that that is what has happened. There are new products that were not there before.

Mr. Hills: With higher profit margins.

Mr. Shenefield: Maybe; I just don't know. I am not investigating it.

Mr. Hills: As a former regulator I have too often seen people reasoning from an assumption. And I just don't know how anybody could assume that it is better to have somebody buy number two or number six. The mere fact that number six has become number two is irrelevant, I think.

MR. SHENEFIELD: I wouldn't agree with that, but I would be interested in talking about it further on the basis of some facts.

LAURENCE SILBERMAN, former deputy attorney general: Mr. Shenefield, I was particularly interested by the discussion earlier between Paul MacAvoy, Roderick Hills, and yourself concerning the rationale you use for looking hard at the concentrated industries for the purpose of generating either a Section 1 or a Section 2 case. Putting aside whatever theory you use once you find what you think is a violation, I would like to go back to the first step. All of us who have been in law enforcement and, perhaps, even our economist friends would agree that the one heinous crime in law enforcement is to direct investigative resources for political purposes; that is to say, to investigate a group or an individual not because that individual or that group is believed to have committed a crime, but rather because of a dislike based on political reasons.

What troubles me about the rationale you use is that it seems to come very close to that, when you concentrate your resources on concentrated industries. It is a double concentration. If Paul MacAvoy is right, and there is no correlation between concentration and illegal activity, then when you direct your investigation of illegal activity at the so-called concentrated industries, you are making a political judgment that these people are really less desirable than others. You decide to go after them to see if you can find a case.

The rationale is that if you do find a case, it will be easier to prove, because there are fewer of these people around. That is not what one would use traditionally as a justification for initiating a law enforcement proceeding. Particularly when you talk about the need to go to Congress to deal with concentrated industries, you are almost implicitly saying, for political reasons, that concentrated industries may be bad, and that is how you justify the resources you put into the investigation of them. Are you troubled by that rationale?

MR. SHENEFIELD: Not in the slightest. I must say that entirely escapes me. For one thing, we are not talking about a crime at all.

MR. SILBERMAN: When you talk about conspiracy we may have a crime.

MR. SHENEFIELD: No. I suppose somebody might conceivably file a criminal action, but I have committed not to do it. It does not seem to me to be responsible to do so. But that is a small quibble, I guess.

MR. SILBERMAN: Just let me stop you for a moment. You certainly would not agree that it is appropriate for the government to file law enforcement actions, whether criminal or not, for political purposes?

MR. SHENEFIELD: Of course not, and I find it a little difficult to follow the logic that equates what I do with a political decision. Of all of the investigation targets open to me, I look in those areas where, first, I think I am likely to find what I am shooting for, and, second, when I find it, I can actually do something about it. I do not understand the criticism.

MR. SILBERMAN: It is a question that turns very much on Paul MacAvoy's point that you are no more likely to find illegal conduct in this group than any other group.

MR. SHENEFIELD: But no less likely.

MR. SILBERMAN: If your economists agree that Paul MacAvoy is right —that you are no more likely to find evidence of illegal conduct in a concentrated industry than in any other—then, it seems to me, a very important threshold question is, Why are you looking particularly at that industry?

MR. SHENEFIELD: But no less likely, sir, no less likely that we will find evidence there.

MR. SILBERMAN: Well, "no less likely" does not justify the priority.

MR. SHENEFIELD: Of course it does.

MR. SILBERMAN: It is no less likely that you will find illegal activity among junk manufacturers. Is that therefore a number one priority?

MR. SHENEFIELD: If I were convinced that, by looking in one group of the population, I could find price fixing and could do something about it, whereas by looking somewhere else I might find it but I couldn't do anything about it, it seems to me silly not to look where I can do something.

PROFESSOR MACAVOY: There must be some basis for developing a coherent and persuasive argument for looking there for price fixers, but not for monopolizers. And if you are looking for monopolizers in the sense of the *American Tobacco* case of 1946,[7] in a sense of conscious parallel action manifest in various kinds of noncompetitive price performance, random selection is better than choosing a block of industries because they happen to be listed at the top of the industrial concentration tables. There are all kinds of reasons built into the numbers for that being a nonrandom process. You are therefore wasting some of those very precious GS-11 resources that way, but that is a quibble.

MR. SHENEFIELD: It would be well, I think, if you could develop a rational argument. I would be interested in seeing it.

PROFESSOR MACAVOY: The more price fixers there are, the more notoriously unsuccessful they are at price fixing. A long tradition in the theory of information built on the work of the Chicago school in the 1960s says it is harder to find chiselers, cheaters, rebaters, and kickbackers in a conspiracy when there are nine than when there are five. A larger number of people means they have an operation in that industry. That is the kind of thing you are looking for and doing very well out there in the hustings.

MR. SHENEFIELD: Not doing very well, but we are doing it.

PROFESSOR MACAVOY: Looking for price fixing in the highly concentrated industries is probably not a good idea because these industries also have the advanced data processing and other information systems that can make everything you are looking for in the files nonexistent. By looking there for the price fixers, you are looking for people who know how to do it without leaving a track. You are in real trouble on that one.

The other side of the argument, however, is that you were really going after those industries because you thought you could win Alcoa-like Section 2 cases.

MR. SHENEFIELD: Are you talking about price fixing now or shared monopoly?

PROFESSOR MACAVOY: Shared monopoly. You have devised a management plan whereby you go to the highly concentrated industries to

[7] American Tobacco Co. v. United States, 328 U.S. 781 (1946).

search for shared monopoly manifestations in price behavior, and then you bring an Alcoa-like case. Now, I do not want to distort what you are saying, but I have a quibble with that management scheme because economic research provides no foundation for it.

MR. SHENEFIELD: The impression is emerging that you don't agree with the procedure. [Laughter.]

I guess this procedure makes as much sense to me as does any other. In fact, it makes more sense for the reasons I have explained a couple of times. By no stretch of the imagination could that be described as a political sort of decision.

PROFESSOR MACAVOY: There is another way of doing it. You just read the newspapers to find the noncompetitive price performance.

MR. SHENEFIELD: It is funny—they turn out to be the same industries.

PROFESSOR MACAVOY: No, they don't.

MR. SHENEFIELD: In my newspaper, they do.

JOHN BARNUM, former deputy secretary of transportation: I perceive that you are proceeding on the premise that a concentrated industry is a bad thing, per se.

MR. SHENEFIELD: No, I said that I might not bring any cases at all. I am not looking only at concentrated industries. That is the way we have started; we have to start somewhere.

MR. BARNUM: Would you not bring the concentrated industry case because you were not able to find the facilitating devices, as you call them, that would support an implicit conspiracy theory? Or would you not bring the concentrated industry case because the economics failed to indicate that the concentration made it less competitive.

MR. SHENEFIELD: The former.

MR. BARNUM: Only the former. Then you agree that you are not bringing only the Section 1 case.

MR. SHENEFIELD: Well, no. It would not even come up unless we could find the second, but the crucial decision will be the first. We will not even be offered the opportunity unless we can have the result. That is why I kept trying to draw a distinction between result and means of achieving it. If we find the result, the next question is, are the means there that we can reach? If they are not there, then we do not bring the case.

MR. BARNUM: I think that the dispute between you and Paul MacAvoy is that he thinks that before you look for facilitating devices for this implicit conspiracy you ought to see whether the economic consequences in the industry are anticompetitive.

MR. SHENEFIELD: Of course. That is why we are going through the process.

PROFESSOR MACAVOY: But that is where the dispute arises. I know thirty-three and a half federal court judges who would find those companies guilty of monopolizing because they are highly concentrated. And I can name the judges that look at performance. There are just four.

MR. SILBERMAN: I challenge you to name the half. [Laughter.]

MR. BARNUM: You say your people are now looking at various industries, and you will get reports early next week, if you haven't them already, as to whether you should be in one of these industries.

Are they bringing you both analyses, that is, the legal analysis of the facilitating devices in this industry, as well as the economic analysis that, indeed, the fact of concentration has led to less price competition and otherwise undesirable economic results?

MR. SHENEFIELD: Neither one; I should not leave you with any misimpression. What I will get next Tuesday is a diagram of how to proceed in order to discover. It seems to me that both analyses will be needed before we make any decision on whether to bring a case. First, is industry X one of those which is operating in a way that could be described as noncompetitive?

MR. BARNUM: Economically or legally under a facilitating device?

MR. SHENEFIELD: Economically. And if we get that, then the question is, how is it achieved? Is it achieved by the facilitating devices? Unless we have both of those, we cannot proceed.

ALAN SELTZER, consultant: Larry Silberman's point is much more relevant than has been generally recognized. You said you were proposing to develop approaches under Section 2. Those were your words. You also said in *U.S. News & World Report* that there is a populist tradition from which the antitrust laws have derived. Since the end of the Civil War, this country has had a strong suspicion of large aggregations of capital. This entirely overlooks the historical tradition of the interpretation of the Sherman Act.

The *U.S. Steel* case of 1920[8] essentially legitimated concentrated industries. The Court's decision was simply accepted by Congress and by the public. Later efforts to deconcentrate industry have not even gotten out of committee. Kaysen and Turner's book[9] proposed the Industrial Reorganization Act, and Senator Philip Hart tried to drum up support for it for years, but it probably does not have any support in the country to speak of, apart from Mark Green and his people. It has never gotten out of committee.

Under these circumstances, can you say that there is not a political effort to proceed against big business? How can you ignore the lack of popular support for deconcentrating industry along Section 2 lines, or the essential legitimation of industrial concentration by the whole tradition of interpreting the rule of reason?

MR. SHENEFIELD: For a couple of reasons: one, because I think concentration does not have much to do with size; two, because I don't view American history the same way you do, and I don't regard Congress or the Supreme Court as a terrifically good substitute for what the people think—certainly, not in this area.

If, as *U.S. News & World Report* does, you were to ask the American people what they think about big business, I am not sure you would get the kind of results you expect. The polls that I read suggest that the American people are fairly suspicious of big business.

MR. SILBERMAN: I don't want to be understood as agreeing with the person who agreed with me. That is to say, I would not think the Antitrust Division was justified in proceeding politically against concentration because a poll suggests the American people believe, at the moment, that that is a popular course of action. That is not my view, and such a poll would not justify that action.

---

[8] United States v. United States Steel Corp., 251 U.S. 417 (1920).

[9] Carl Kaysen and Donald F. Turner, *Antitrust Policy: An Economic and Legal Analysis* (Cambridge, Mass.: Harvard University Press, 1959).

Mr. Shenefield: I guess my confusion over your question is because you slid so quickly from a discussion of shared monopoly into a discussion of the wellsprings of the antitrust laws. I am convinced, from reading the antitrust laws and from reading the views of people who have interpreted them, that there is—not exclusively, but partially—a tradition of suspicion of bigness.

I would argue strongly that no case filed in recent years has been based on that suspicion of bigness. There are no cases filed that do not make economic sense; when filed, they were viewed as having made perfectly good economic sense or they would not have been filed. And I would not argue that lack of success of a particular bill in any committee in Congress has much to do with what the American people think about that proposition. I would be interested in any views you have on that subject.

Professor Zeckhauser: You were billed as a deregulator, and many of us believe that much regulation has taken place in industries that are naturally quite competitive. I was heartened to hear of your work in the energy department. I know a little bit about collaboration with the Civil Aeronautics Board. If we really want to get effective deregulation in some of these areas where we may have created an industry more concentrated than would be natural, we probably have to promise the American public, or the Congress, or whomever to be vigilant in the antitrust area.

Except in the rare case of someone like Alfred Kahn of the CAB, however, I can't see your natural allies within the regulatory agencies saying, "We thought we were serving the public interest. Actually, we didn't have our theory quite straight. We are going out of business, but we are leaving a fairly concentrated industry. We want you to take over our responsibilities and make sure the firms do compete the way economists say they are going to."

Can you think of a scenario, other than an occasional fortuitous event as in the case of the CAB, where this could happen to any great extent, or is this just pie in the sky? Will you have to limit yourself to preventing new regulations from further discouraging competition, as you suggest might be the case in the energy area?

Mr. Shenefield: No, I think a couple of things might happen. There is nothing new about discrete filings and discrete interventions which have some results of that sort. In addition—I would again be interested in the reaction of people here—a statute has been proposed by Senator Kennedy, the so-called Competition Improvements Act, S.2028. It will probably be substantially slimmed down and proposed again. It would require regulators to make decisions that are, in effect, a rule of reason. In the event that a decision is not consistent with a competitive choice, they make the least anticompetitive decision they can; and the decision must serve some important social policy that the regulators can articulate and that is all spelled out.

I suppose that might produce much more cumbersome regulatory proceedings. It could also force attention to the competitive principle in a particular decision. I don't know. What do you all think from your experience in this area? Do you think such a thing at the Securities and Exchange Commission might have made or might make a difference?

MR. HILLS: Almost anything that makes regulators think does some good sometimes, but I don't mean to be quite that facetious.

MR. SHENEFIELD: It is very difficult for a regulator to substitute different tests for the statutory test he is obliged to fulfill. A subjective standard almost always leads to some mischief because it allows the regulator to avoid his primary statutory mandate, which is subject to some sort of judicial review. The regulator can say, "Well, I didn't do what I am supposed to do because of this other consideration." An obligation to do something in the public interest is fairly vague. The Competition Improvements Act purports, at least, to flesh that out a bit and give judges a little better handle.

MR. SILBERMAN: You are not serious!

MR. HILLS: It is a long way down the road from, say, the SEC, which is a fairly sophisticated agency and still struggling to find the economic consequences of its own actions. To throw from left field some catch word that the agency does not have the capacity to deal with diverts it from what it is doing. We testified against that bill, not because we did not think we should seek more competition but because our objective at the SEC, for example, is either to permit some activity to occur or not to permit it to occur under the statute that the SEC has been given. To use a totally different test—to say that in every single case the least anticompetitive alternatives must be determined—puts two traditions totally at odds. It is a patch job. There is no way in the world that an agency could go through the regulatory process, come to a decision, and then look around and say, "But here is another decision with a less anticompetitive result." The illogic of it is terrifying.

MR. SHENEFIELD: You don't think that what Fred Kahn has done at the CAB has changed the balance of the principles a little?

MR. HILLS: Not at all, no. I think and hope that Fred Kahn has paid attention to a great deal of economic data, which said this kind of protection was not needed, that the public interest was not served by monopolies and by less competition.

MR. SILBERMAN: When Fred Kahn was here at AEI he almost admitted that if he were a lawyer he couldn't have done what he did. He thought what he was doing made sound economic sense, but he was bothered about whether it deviated from his statutory mandate. It did trouble him, and legitimately.

DR. MILLER: At the time that S.2028 came up, I think, Mr. Hills was still in the White House, and the administration decided to testify in support of it. Then Mr. Hills changed jobs, and testified against it. Is that right?

MR. SILBERMAN: Where you stand depends on where you sit?

MR. HILLS: No, we supported a stronger position. I think the Office of Management and Budget came out with an entirely different point, which was to test the economic capacity of these agencies, to strike at their original charter and not give the agency an alternative test.

MR. COLLIER: S.2028 leaves vague the definition of competition. Many people say we ought to write regulations to disadvantage large firms and to advantage small ones. But it seems to me that it is not going to move the ball very much to write a safety regulation that tries to enhance competition by exempting every firm under 100 employees. My own experience convinces me that most regulators, given that language and nothing more, would simply believe that they had to exclude small firms or to write standards so that small firms could comply with them. The problem with that approach is that there is a basic misunderstanding of what competition is.

MR. SHENEFIELD: It is clearly a problem. I guess I am not quite as pessimistic about that language, because it is being worked out in a number of regulatory agencies—not in the form of a statutory amendment, but through filings made by your former agency and the one that I head.

I guess I also rely on appellate review—I don't think any judge would accede to that as a proper obligation.

Mr. Collier: The energy area is a good example. Often people claim that competition is involved when, in fact, what is involved is small entities.

Mr. Hills: There is something very real to be accomplished here, particularly in the regulatory agencies. I think that Senator Kennedy's staff came to the conclusion that it was, in the long run, more harmful than helpful to deal with it without amending the fundamental charter of the agency, that it was better not to give them an alternative test but to spend a little more time, another session or two, and dig out the fundamental charter of the agency.

Mr. Collier: The National Commission on the Review of Antitrust Laws and Procedures has been addressing many of the areas that you have mentioned, John. It has been working now for four or five months, and your deadline is coming up. What, at this point, do you see coming out of that work as useful recommendations on complex litigation, deregulation, or the antitrust exemptions? There is also some question whether the statutes—the Sherman Act—ought to be tinkered with.

Mr. Shenefield: For those of you who haven't been keeping up with it, the executive order directed the commission to look at two different areas, expedition of complex antitrust litigation, on the one hand, and the desirability of retaining antitrust exemptions and immunities, on the other. The executive order also fixed a six-month life for the commission. Let me summarize briefly where the commission seems to be headed.

In the area of expediting complex litigation there will be a number of procedural recommendations, in all likelihood, that may sound insignificant but that I think will prove to be quite significant. They have to do with panels of judges, with initial pretrial conference with masters and magistrates, with deadlines, and discovery, and control of litigation. Those will all be technical suggestions about amendments to the rules of civil procedure and the like.

There is, as part of that general effort, some interest in the commission in considering changes in the statute. There have been proposals to change the attempted monopolization section of Section 2 of the Sherman Act, at least in suits by the government. It is unclear what the commission will do about that.

Professor Flynn has proposed that some kind of "innocent monopolist" statute be enacted. It is unclear what the commission will do about that.

MR. HILLS: There are a lot of exemptions to this.

MR. SHENEFIELD: Yes, in the area of exemptions and immunities, we are spending more time on trucking than anything else.

My guess is that recommendations will range from the very specific to the general and hortatory. If there are going to be any specific recommendations at all, they will come in the area of trucking. I would expect to see a fairly strong, detailed pro-deregulation statement from the commission in the area of trucking, with more general statements about deregulation in some other areas—possibly insurance, possibly Capper-Volstead,[10] possible Webb[11]—and maybe some statement in favor of something like S. 2028.

DR. MILLER: I want to end with the question you asked earlier: Why do we have the merger movement? John Barnum has just given a speech, entitled "The Urge to Merge," in which he develops a fascinating point that I would like him to articulate.

MR. BARNUM: As I was looking at why there is this wave of mergers, I came across something that Professor William Fellner here at AEI has done. He has taken the Federal Reserve data and come up with the following analysis: in the present stock market—to answer the classical question whether it is better to "make" or to buy companies—it is cheaper to buy. The stock market value of all nonfinancial corporations in the United States today is 55 percent of the equity value of those corporations, calculated in terms of the replacement cost of the assets, less the debt. Even if one pays a 100 percent premium or a 50 percent premium over present stock market value, it is possible

[10] The Capper-Volstead Act of 1922 extended Section 6 of the Clayton Act to exempt capital stock agricultural cooperatives.

[11] The Webb Act extended antitrust exemption to "agreements or acts in the course of export trade by an association entered into for the sole purpose of engaging in such trade."

to acquire replacement cost values in excess of the price paid in the stock market.

That paradox is inconsistent with one of the reasons people do this. People go the "buy route" rather than the "make route" because they can quickly fold a going business into their own balance sheet and do not need to go through all the very difficult noneconomic regulatory barriers to starting up a new business or even to expanding their present business—whether those barriers be environmental, toxicological, or safety and health.

DR. MILLER: But there is a dilemma here. If there are rents to an existing firm because they have the certificate of public convenience and necessity to dump into the water, or to pollute the air, or whatever, the stock value should far exceed the asset value. That is the paradox and needs to be explained.

MR. HILLS: Mr. Barnum left out one of his points, which was that one's own equity is also undervalued; therefore one does not have access to capital that would be useful when buying.

PROFESSOR MACAVOY: So there should be no wave of mergers. [Laughter.]

DR. MILLER: Your presentation was greatly enjoyed, and I hope that you will feel free to come back and visit us again. Thank you.

MR. SHENEFIELD: I have enjoyed being here. Thank you very much.